W9-ABM-140

A Chameleon's Life

by Ellen Lawrence

Consultants:

Stephen Hammack
Terrestrial Ectotherm Keeper, Fort Worth Zoo, Fort Worth, Texas

Kelli Hammack
Herpetological Institute for Scientific Study (HISS), Fort Worth, Texas

Kimberly Brenneman, PhD
National Institute for Early Education Research, Rutgers University, New Brunswick, New Jersey

New York, New York

Credits

Cover, © Chris Mattison/FLPA and © Chris Mattison/FLPA; 3, © Winfried Schäfer/Imagebroker/FLPA; 4TR, © Imagebroker.net/Superstock; 4–5, © Jurgen & Christine Sohns/FLPA; 7, © Vincent Grafhorst/Minden Pictures/FLPA; 9T, © Winfried Schäfer/Imagebroker/FLPA; 9B, © Thomas Marent/Visuals Unlimited Ltd/Getty Images; 10, © Bill Love/Blue Chameleon Ventures; 11, © Premaphotos/Alamy; 12T, © Cyril Ruoso/Minden Pictures/FLPA; 12B, © Gerry Ellis/Minden Pictures/FLPA; 13, © Arco Images GmbH/Alamy; 14–15, © Chris Mattison/FLPA; 16, © National Geographic Image Collection/Alamy; 16–17, © Jurgen & Christine Sohns/FLPA; 18 BL, © M. Dykstra/Shutterstock; 18 BM, © irin-k/Shutterstock; 18 BL Ultrashock/Shutterstock; 18–19, © Thomas Marent/Minden Pictures/FLPA; 19B, © Winfried Schäfer/Imagebroker/FLPA; 20–21, © Hugh Lansdown/FLPA and © Winfried Schäfer/Imagebroker/FLPA; 22TL, © Rich Carey/Shutterstock; 22ML, © Norbert Nagel/Wikipedia Creative Commons; 22MR, © Matt Jeppson/Shutterstock; 22BL, © Istomina Olena/Shutterstock; 22BR, © Eric Isselée/Shutterstock; 23TL, © Claudia Naerdemann/Shutterstock; 23TC, © Chris Mattison/FLPA; 23TR, © Tyler Fox/Shutterstock; 23BL, © Stayer/Shutterstock; 23BC, © Vincent Grafhorst/Minden Pictures/FLPA; 23BR, © Hugh Lansdown/Shutterstock.

Publisher: Kenn Goin
Senior Editor: Lisa Wiseman
Creative Director: Spencer Brinker
Design: Alix Wood
Editor: Mark J. Sachner
Photo Researcher: Ruby Tuesday Books Ltd

Library of Congress Cataloging-in-Publication Data

Lawrence, Ellen, 1967–
A chameleon's life / by Ellen Lawrence.
p. cm. — (Animal diaries: life cycles)
Includes bibliographical references and index.
ISBN 978-1-61772-596-8 (library binding) — ISBN 1-61772-596-X (library binding)
1. Chameleons—Life cycles—Juvenile literature. I. Title.
QL666.L23L39 2013
597.95'6—dc23
2012012184

For more information, write to Bearport Publishing Company, Inc., 45 West 21st Street, Suite 3B, New York, New York 10010. Printed in the United States of America.

10 9 8 7 6 5 4 3 2 1

Contents

Name: Sylvie Date: February 1

Watching Chameleons

Today, I watched panther chameleons climb in the trees near my house.

Chameleons are a kind of **lizard**.

I live on Madagascar, a big island in the Indian Ocean.

It's the only place in the world where panther chameleons live in the wild.

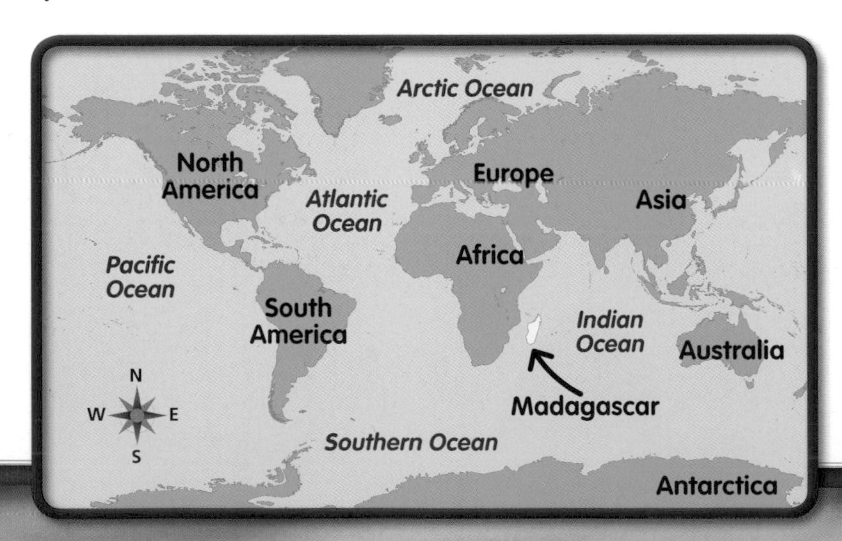

Where panther chameleons live in the wild

From nose to tail, male panther chameleons grow up to 20 inches (51 cm) long. Females grow to about 10 inches (25 cm) long.

Make a list of wild animals that live in your neighborhood. How many can you think of? Which ones do you like best? Why?

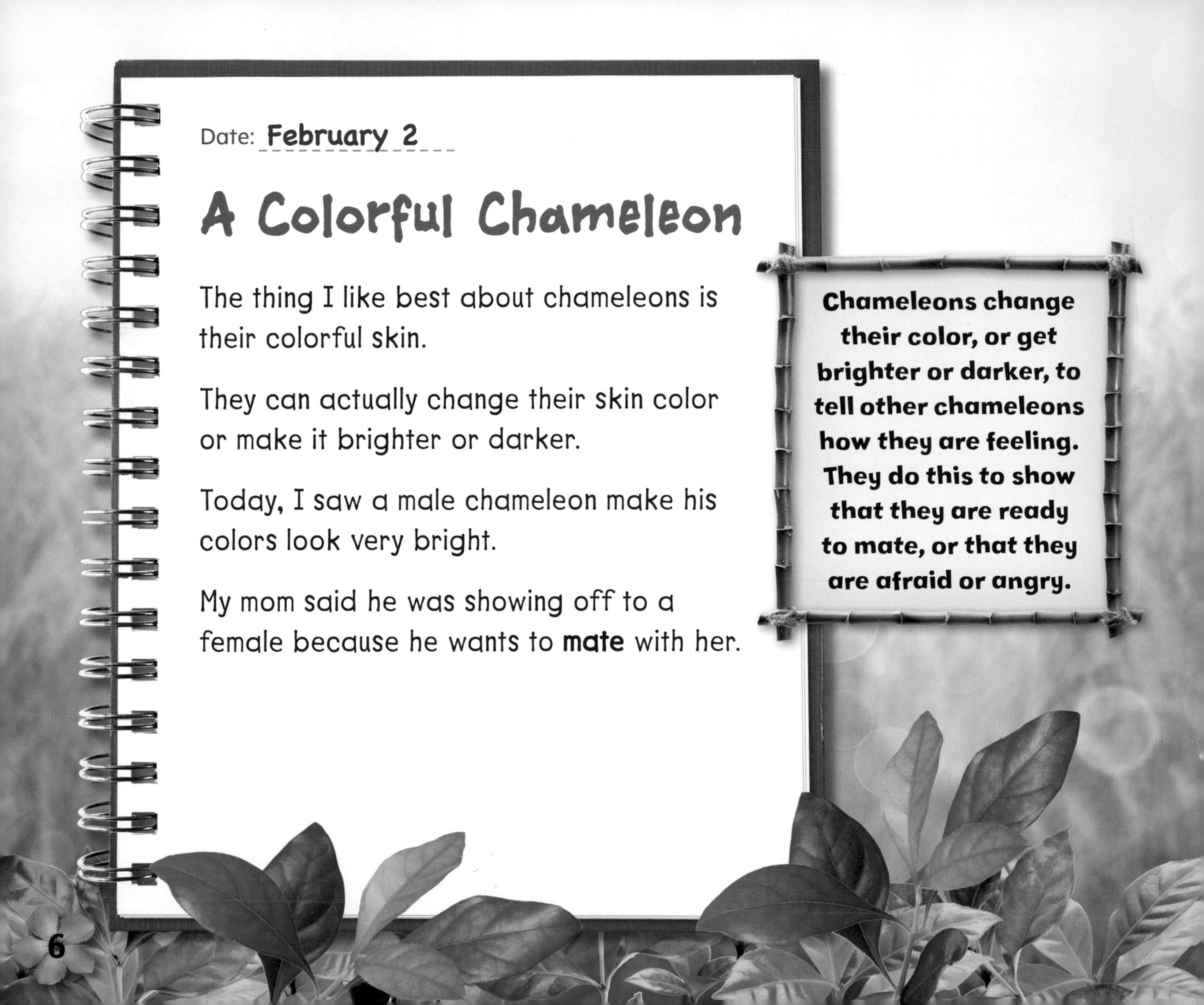

Date: February 2

A Colorful Chameleon

The thing I like best about chameleons is their colorful skin.

They can actually change their skin color or make it brighter or darker.

Today, I saw a male chameleon make his colors look very bright.

My mom said he was showing off to a female because he wants to **mate** with her.

Chameleons change their color, or get brighter or darker, to tell other chameleons how they are feeling. They do this to show that they are ready to mate, or that they are afraid or angry.

Look at the male chameleon in this picture. List all the different colors you can see on his skin.

Date: **February 4**

An Important Sign

The male and female chameleons mated two days ago.

Before she mated, the female had brown skin with pale orange patches.

Now, the patches on her skin have turned bright orange.

This color change tells other males that she has mated and they shouldn't bother her.

It also means that she is getting ready to lay her eggs!

Panther chameleons belong to an animal group called reptiles. Reptiles are cold-blooded and have a backbone and scaly skin. Many female reptiles lay eggs.

female chameleon before mating
female chameleon after mating

Date: **February 23**

Chameleon Eggs

It's been almost three weeks since the chameleons mated.

Chameleons usually spend most of their time in trees.

Today, however, the female climbed down to the ground.

She dug a hole under the tree's branches and laid her eggs in it.

Then she filled the hole with dirt and placed leaves and twigs on top of it.

Why do you think the female chameleon covered the place where she'd laid her eggs with leaves and twigs?

Female panther chameleons lay between 10 and 50 eggs at one time.

Date: March 30

Chameleon Predators

After the chameleon buried her eggs, she climbed back up into the tree.

Mother chameleons don't look after their eggs or their babies once the eggs **hatch**.

That's why the chameleon covered the place where she laid her eggs.

She didn't want **predators** such as snakes and civets to find the eggs and eat them.

It's been almost five weeks and no other animals have found her hiding place.

The colors of a chameleon's skin allow it to blend in with the trees where it lives. This helps a chameleon hide from predators such as birds and snakes.

Date: **September 20**

The Babies Hatch!

It's been almost seven months since the chameleon laid her eggs.

Today, I saw something amazing—a tiny baby chameleon.

It had hatched from its egg and climbed up through the soil.

I watched all afternoon, and I saw 20 babies in total pop up from underground!

What do you think the chameleon babies will do next?

A baby chameleon may hatch from its egg after six months. It can take as long as 13 months, though.

baby chameleon hatching
egg

Date: **September 21**

Climbing Babies

The parents of baby chameleons aren't around to protect them.

So, the babies quickly climbed up into the trees to hide among the leaves.

Chameleons are very good at climbing.

They have five toes with claws on each foot.

They use their toes to grip the tree branches.

If they need to climb up or down a smooth tree trunk, they use their claws to hold on.

a chameleon's toes

A newly hatched panther chameleon measures about 1.5 inches (3.8 cm) from its nose to the tip of its tail.
baby panther chameleon

Date: October 1

A Superfast Snacker!

Both baby and adult chameleons catch **insects**.

Today, I saw one of the young chameleons catch a fly.

The chameleon shot its long tongue out of its mouth.

The fly stuck to the tongue's sticky end and then the chameleon ate it.

It all happened in less than a second!

Panther chameleons eat many different insects including these:

cockroach

fly

butterfly

A panther chameleon's long tongue is about one and a half times the length of its body!

a chameleon eating a dragonfly

Date: **December 20**

Growing Up

The baby chameleons are now three months old.

They still have their brown skin color.

Soon, the males will turn blue or green, and the females will grow orange patches.

When they are six months old, the chameleons will be adults and ready to mate.

I can't wait to see the chameleons have babies of their own!

Panther chameleons usually live for about two years.

Science Lab

Panther chameleons and all other lizards are reptiles.

Reptiles have a backbone, scaly skin, and they are cold-blooded.

Snakes, turtles, tortoises, crocodiles, and alligators are also reptiles.

Be a Reptile Scientist

Write a report comparing a panther chameleon to another reptile.

You can choose one of the reptiles on this page or pick one of your favorites.

Then use the Internet and books to research the animal's life.

Answer these questions in your report:

What does the reptile you've chosen look like?

Where does it live?

What does it eat?

How is it similar to and different from the chameleon?

sea turtle

desert tortoise

alligator

iguana lizard

corn snake

Science Words

cold-blooded (KOHLD-*bluhd*-id) having a body temperature that goes up or down to match the temperature of the air or water around the body

hatch (HACH) to break out of an egg

insects (IN-sekts) small animals that have six legs, two antennas, a hard covering called an exoskeleton, and three main body parts

lizard (LIZ-urd) a cold-blooded animal with a backbone, scaly skin, four legs, and a tail

mate (MAYT) to come together in order to have young

predators (PRED-uh-turz) animals that hunt and eat other animals

Index

Read More

Bishop, Nic. *Lizards.* New York: Scholastic Inc (2010).

Shea, Therese. *Creepy Reptiles (Nature's Creepiest Creatures).* New York: Gareth Stevens Publishing (2012).

Squire, Ann O. *Chinese Giant Salamander (SuperSized!).* New York: Bearport Publishing (2007).

Learn More Online

To learn more about chameleons, visit **www.bearportpublishing.com/AnimalDiaries**

About the Author

Ellen Lawrence lives in the United Kingdom. Her favorite books to write are those about animals. In fact, the first book Ellen bought for herself, when she was six years old, was the story of a gorilla named Patty Cake that was born in New York's Central Park Zoo.